Self-Discipline

Habits and Exercises to Develop Discipline and a Willpower That Will Make You More Successful

Harvey Segler

FREE Bonus!

Want to make money while you sleep?

Visit >>>www.GreenSleeper.com<<< to get free tips about how you can make serious money while doing anything else! Sleeping, laying on the beach, traveling, only your imagination is the limit!

At the moment you can get a FREE download of:

The "Make Money While You Sleep" Guide

But hurry up, the book will not be there forever!

Visit My Friends Website And Download It Now! 100% Free! What Do You Have To Lose? Just visit www.GreenSleeper.com.

If you don't want the book, read the blog which can teach you a lot of things about business, time management, performance and other things connected to business and success.

Table of contents

Introduction

I want to thank you and congratulate you for getting the book, *Self-Discipline - Habits and Exercises to Develop Discipline and a Willpower That Will Make You More Successful.*

This book contains proven steps and strategies on how to lead a more successful life through self-discipline. In the modern day in which we live, we all wish to be successful. Either we are working jobs that we hate, or we are wishing that we could move on and better ourselves, or we want to lose weight, or achieve this or that, and the list goes on.

Yet, we want our freedom. We want to do what we want. We want to do it when we want to. The sound of a schedule, and more work, and greater restrictions, all make the idea of self-discipline sound like a bad idea.

But it isn't. It is through the concept of self-discipline that you are going to enjoy a freedom that is unlike any that you have ever felt before. You are going to find that you really can do what you want and you can also be successful in life.

You are going to learn how to discipline yourself, and your schedule to have time for what you want to do, and still have time for more. And not only that, but I am going to show you how you can sharpen your willpower into what you need to be successful in this life.

The people who are on top are the people that are willing to work for it, and if you are going to work for it, you are going to need to know how to do that and still have time for the life that you love.

This book is going to show you everything you need to know to learn that self-discipline and sharpen that willpower. So open your mind and get ready, you are going to learn a whole new way to approach your day, and no matter what it is you want to be more successful in, you are going to achieve your dream, and enjoy that success you have been longing for!

It is then that you are going to realize what true freedom is, and it is going to rock your world.

Thanks again for getting this book, I hope you enjoy it!

Chapter 1 – Your Greatest Fight is against Yourself

Problems. They are everywhere. They could be blatant problems such as health problems or money issues, work related issues or a failing relationship. You think that you are doing everything right, and everything that you need to do, but it seems like it is all falling apart around you.

Of course, this doesn't make much sense. You are doing what you want, and you have the partner that you want. You have the job that you want. You work, but you can take time off when you want. You do the hobbies that you want and you eat what you want. On paper, life is really good.

But we aren't living life on paper, and you aren't truly happy. Oh sure, you are doing things that are going to medicate your unhappiness. You might drink or smoke or see people that you want to see, or you might be 'wild and free' and drift from job to job, which makes you think you are happy, but when it comes down to the heart of the matter, you aren't happy with your life.

There's that gnawing feeling that something is missing, or that you could be better at this or do better at that. You might want to look different, or have a more fulfilling relationship, or make more money, but no matter how hard you try, you aren't getting any closer to that goal.

So why bother, right?

I want you to close your eyes for a minute, and imagine a dark road. It is paved, and there are yellow lines dotting the center. It is a still night with the moon and stars out, and there are lamp lights that are lining the road so you can see.

You are the only one out here, and you are running. You are running fast and hard. The end is in sight, but it is a good ways down the road in front of you. You are out of breath, and you feel worn.

You want to give up. Toss in the towel and walk away.

"Who cares?" You ask yourself.

Then the little voices inside of you start to pipe up with their own opinions.

"I'm tired."

"It's too hard."

"This is uncomfortable."

There are so many reasons that you can think of that drain simply the motivation right out of you. The more you think about it, the less you want to actually finish, and the more you want to give up.

Sounds a little bit like the situations you are dealing with in life, doesn't it?

I want to share with you now a paraphrased quote by Will Smith.

"When you are running, there is a little person inside of you that is saying, 'I'm tired. My lungs are about to pop.

I'm so hurt there is no way I can possibly continue.' And you want to quit.

If you learn how to defeat that person while you are running, you will learn how not to quit. Even when things get hard in your life, you will keep pushing on."

It's true. We have hard times in life, and it is the immediate reaction to give up. We hear that little voice inside of us that is telling us we want to quit, walk away, and not give it another thought. Who cares about how this comes out? I am going to just walk away... the most common attitude for many people who are dealing with hard times.

But I am telling you now that you have to learn to defeat that little voice. That voice may be asking you *who cares if you finish the race,* but I am telling you that *you care if you finish.*

All too often in life we are faced with difficulties, and we give up. We want to be successful, but hard things come and bad things happen, and we are the first to toss our hands in the air and announce that "no one cares, so why bother?"

There is that little voice inside of all of us that is telling us to focus on the wrong things in life. This is the voice that fuels our desire to have our own way all the time, to put ourselves first in every situation, and to do what we want.

It is the voice that tells us to break the rules, and to not be bound by schedules or by doing anything that doesn't line up with what we want to do. It is the voice that tells you that in order to be free you have to go through life "looking out for number one."

Consider this voice to be everything that you don't want to be. Sure, you want to be free, and you do want to do what you want, but this voice is lying to you. It is feeding you a twisted version of freedom that isn't true freedom, and it is, in essence, preventing you from having the life that you want.

Now, you may be feeling like you do have the life that you want, minus the level of success you are hoping for, but I don't think you do. I feel like you are making the best out of the life that you have, but you aren't living the life that you want.

There is a definite difference here, and it is all the difference between a life of slavery to your desires, and a life of freedom, and a life of failure versus a life of success.

Discipline. Discipline is the answer.

Now, if you are like most people, the word 'discipline' has a negative connotation to it. You assume that it is going to be something bad, and that you aren't going to like it. It is going to be time consuming, it is going to require a lot of work, and it is going to take away from you the things that you want to do.

All in all, this is a word that you thought you grew out of when you moved out of your parents' house, and it is not something that you are too willing to jump back in to.

After all, you are an adult, right? This means that you are free to do what you want. Total freedom, no rules, no wrong, just what you want when you want. That is the dream, right?

If that is true... then why are you here? Why aren't you as happy in your relationship as you could be? Why aren't you as successful as you want to be? Why aren't you... well... happy?

You have a list of things that you want to change about yourself, but you want to change them the fast and easy way, you want to take that magic bullet of a pill that is going to make you look like you want to look, make your partner love you like you want them to, and give you all of the money and possessions that you could ever want.

Surely there is a way that you can have these things... without that dreaded word 'discipline' hanging over your head.

You need to change your feelings and negative emotions towards discipline, and you are going to unleash the key to your happiness, your success, and moving forward in your life.

That voice that is telling you that you can't do it because it is too hard, is a voice that is undisciplined. I know that this doesn't sound like fun right now, but I am going to show you how wonderful your life can be once you embrace this word.

It is going to take some time and effort, but if you are serious about success, you are going to make it. It is just going to take some time.

Not many people realize that they are the ones that are holding themselves back from success. They blame all kinds of outward things, and fail to look within themselves. They don't realize that it is their own selfish desires that are holding them back from a life of success and happiness.

I know this all sounds strange right now, but once it is explained, you are going to understand. You need to win this battle that is against yourself, and you need to learn how to control yourself. This is going to lead you to a life of freedom and success, and make you happier than you could ever imagine.

You are strong, and you are capable... so what are going waiting for? In the chapters to come I am going to show you how you can defeat that little voice inside of you, and how you can take control of your life.

You do have the capability to be successful, you just have to work for it.

Chapter 2 – How to Live a Successful Life: Part 1

It is no secret that we all wish to be successful in life. No kid dreams of growing up to become unsuccessful and live a life of stress and barely making ends meet. Now, that isn't to say that every kid wishes to grow up to become a millionaire, but as kids we all wanted to grow up to have enough.

The plan was to grow up and get a job, and a house, and maybe get married, and have our own kids. Most of us wanted to have fancy and nice things, and it wasn't at all an uncommon thought to have as much as we ever could want.

We never thought of where all of this success was coming from, we just automatically assumed that we would have it. Sure, we were willing to work, but again our idea of work was a lot different when we were kids than it is now that we are actually living it.

Be honest with yourself. Are you doing right now what you always said you wanted to do when you were a kid? Did you really think you were going to grow up to become a (fill in the blank)?

Not to say that there is anything wrong with what you do for a living, you might actually enjoy it, but that is not the point. My point is that you wanted to be successful, and as you are reading a book to help you gain greater success, you aren't as successful as you once thought you would be by this time in your life.

So what are you going to do about it?

Clearly, change it. You want to be successful, so I am going to tell you how to do it. Be warned, you may not like what you read at first, but bear with me, and I am going to show you how you really can be successful and happy in your life.

The key to success

Each and every one of us craves freedom. That is something that has been a part of man since the dawn of time, and it is something that we continue to seek after today.

We want freedom in our time, in our relationships, in our work... in just about anything that we do in a day. We don't want to be told what to do by anyone, and we certainly don't want to have to do anything that is not our idea in the first place.

Sound familiar? More than likely it does. If you are a free thinking person, it is very likely you fall into the realm of a freedom seeker. You want to do what you want when you want, and no one can tell you otherwise.

In addition to that, you want to be successful. This is perfectly normal, everyone in life wants to be successful, but then you balk at what they say you have to do to get there.

Clearly you are looking for advice on how to become more successful in life. That is the main purpose of this book here, but you may not be too thrilled with the idea that is behind the success... at least not yet anyway.

If you have done any research into the realm of success, you have probably noticed a trend.

It requires a lot of work.

You need to devote time to growing within yourself, you need to open up to the people around you, you need to be efficient and work hard when you are at work. You need to do this, and more of that, and less of this, and the list goes on.

But hold on just a second... I don't want to be a slave to a schedule... I want to be free. I can't have my day eaten up with meetings and conversations or hours of meditation and personal growth. I want to be successful on *my* schedule.

If your reaction was anything like this, don't worry, you aren't alone. Many people out there wish to be successful, but the same number of people out there are also happy with their freedom.

They feel that if they are to commit to a rigid schedule then they are giving up their freedom, and nobody wants to do that.

"I just want to be able to do what I want when I want to do it. I am not an overly religious person, I'm not one of those people that is always looking for the higher and the greater or the deeper, I'm just someone that wants success in life." You may be thinking this very thing right now, and the sound of what I said you need to do to be successful isn't all that appealing.

But you know what? That's ok. I understand where you are coming from, and I understand you.

You are looking for something that is fun, adventurous, exciting... freedom really.

I am about to tell you something that is going to shake your world, however.

You are not going to become successful... in fact you are not going to even have the freedom that you so deeply crave... with the way you are currently living life.

Surprised? Don't be.

Let me explain to you why this is true.

Chapter 3 – Stop Complicating the Simple

Right now your thoughts must be racing. How can you give up freedom to gain more freedom? How can you not be free when you are doing what you want? How are you supposed to have the time to do more things when you already feel like you don't have time to do what you already need to do?

I know how much of a shock this is at first, and I understand why you are feeling frustrated about it, but I am going to challenge you to think about your life in a new light. Perhaps you have a backwards view of things, and you are inadvertently making your life harder than it needs to be.

There are many things in life that sneak up on us under the guise that they are helping us, when they are really serving to make our lives harder than they need to be. For instance, that little chip that they are putting in your debit card is supposed to make your life a lot easier. You are now going to have more security, payment is supposed to be faster, and the list goes on.

But what happens when you go to use it at the store? You find that the card machine doesn't like the chip, or that it takes longer than if you were to do it like you always did before. Not to say that they won't make them faster down the road, but right now this 'convenience' is really robbing of a lot of time.

And cards aren't the only thing in life that do this. We are consumed with the 'easy' way of doing things. We want what we want right now. Why wait when we can have it today? You only live once... the common thought patterns of today's world, but consider this, in our quest to do the easy thing, we are really making our lives a lot harder.

Think of it this way:

"The easy thing is the hard thing, and the hard thing is the easy thing."

I know this sounds contradictory right now, but let me explain. Most people want what is easy. They want the fun, the excitement, the reward... all right now. They don't want to do what is long and hard if they can do what is quick and easy to get what they want.

Of course, I agree. Why would you want to waste your time on something that is going to take you time and hard work when you can get the same result a lot faster another way? But this is where the catch is.

Consider this: what if you wanted to achieve peace of mind. You are stressed out, you are tired, you are worried. Your mind is cluttered with all kinds of thoughts and fears and outside things that just run all hope of peace out the window.

So you do some research, and what you learn is that in order to achieve peace of mind, you need to meditate for a few hours a day for a decade.

Suddenly, alarms are going off inside your head. You tell yourself that you would be miserable if you did that, and that there is no way you would ever do that. You refuse to try for peace of mind in this way, so what do you do? You go about it another way.

You go do doctors. You take trips. You take medication, you try this, and you try that and everything else that comes to your mind... all because they promise that you will achieve the peace of mind faster.

But what happens?

Nothing. You are still struggling with a mind that is in torment, and nothing that you are doing is helping.

Yes, it might be difficult for you to set aside a few hours a day to meditate, which makes that a hard thing to do. But if you are spending all of this time trying all of the quick and easy fixes with no results, then you are working a lot harder on the so called 'easy things'.

As you can see here, it would have been better for you to have gone with the 'hard' method of meditation in the beginning, and skip all of the so called easy things that aren't getting you anywhere.

Let's take a minute and do some self-examination. Now, I know that this isn't fun, and that you would like to see yourself as you want to be instead of how you currently are, but this is a great way to grow, and to explore how you can change into what you really do want to be.

Are you happy with your life as it is, and where you are right now?

Now I am not asking if you are happy in general, that may be yes or no, but it has no bearing on what I am really talking about.

- Are you happy with where your life is headed?

- Are you accomplishing the goals that you want to accomplish?

- Are you achieving your dreams?

- Is there something, or maybe a few things, that you wish you could do?

- Do you feel like you would do more if you had the time?

- Do you struggle with getting everything done on the time that you have?

- Do you feel stressed, or like you are stuck in life?

If you answered yes to any of these questions, I challenge you to ask yourself how well your method of 'freedom' is working for you.

Ask yourself if you have a choice in life. Are you doing what you want to do with your life, and if you aren't could you change it? Or do you really feel like you have no choice?

It is ironic that so many people shy away from scheduling and putting pressure on themselves because they don't want to give up their freedom, but once they examine their lives in the light of true freedom, they find that they really aren't very free at all.

It won't take much effort at all to realize that while you think you are in control of your desires, you are actually a puppet that is being controlled by your desires.

You want to be the one that is calling all of the shots. You want to do what you want when you want, but when it comes down to the heart of the matter, you are really scared to change anything that you are doing, because you are afraid to give up any of your wants.

Right now, you think that you are free. You think that you have the freedom to eat whatever you want. Because you are not going to eat what 'health nuts' say you should eat.

You think you have the freedom to be lazy in your relationship because you love her or him and they aren't going to leave you.

You think that you have the freedom to be lazy at work, or to call in at any time that you please, because you are wild and free and you aren't going to be bound by anyone else's schedule.

For you, this is all fun and new and exciting. You like being a rebel and not having to follow the rules.

But I have news for you... living like this isn't freedom.

You may call yourself a 'free spirit' or someone that isn't going to follow what anyone else says, but what you think is this unprecedented realm of freedom, is actually a slave driver to you.

You don't have freedom in this way of life, you are a slave to your desires. They rule you. Every whim and every fancy that pops into your brain, you *have* to do whether it is good for you or not. There are consequences to the choices that you are making, and more often than not, they aren't good.

Your relationship ends. You don't get that promotion, or worse, you lose your job all together. You gain weight or you deal with health issues. All of this so called freedom is leading you down a path of destructions... which really doesn't sound like freedom to me at all.

Odds are, if you are living this kind of life, you aren't happy.

I wish it really were that easy to live a happy life. To get up in the morning and say "I don't feel like going to work, so I'm not going to," and have no consequences for it at all.

I have to tell you, if it were that easy, we all would be doing it, but it's not. Through many years of learning things the hard way, I have learned that you have to be a lot more strategic about a lot of things in life if you want to be successful, if you want to be happy, and if you want to have that peace of mind.

While you may think that 'getting or doing everything you want is the key to happiness' it really isn't.

There is good news, however, that I am going to share with you now.

You *can* take control of your life, and you *can* be in control of your desires. You really can have and do what you want and be successful, all at the same time. Even better than that, you can have more freedom than you have now, even more freedom than you ever thought you could have, once you are willing to discipline yourself.

I know that sounds like backwards thinking, and like I am going to trick you into giving up the freedom that you have, but I promise you I am not. In the chapters to come, I am going to show you how you can enjoy more freedom than you ever have before, by putting rigidity and a schedule on yourself.

What you are experiencing now isn't real freedom, but I am going to show you what real freedom is, and how you can have it for yourself. So let go of any misconceptions you have about the idea of discipline, and read on with an open mind.

It is going to change your life in more ways than you can imagine.

Chapter 4 – The Problem With "Do What You Want" Thinking

We all know that person, or knew that person, or maybe *you* were that person... the one that proclaims himself or herself to be a 'free spirit' and as such is completely free. They are that person that may or may not have a job, but more frequently is that person that sometimes has a job.

They will do this through the summer than drift through something else through the winter. They might go back to one thing again, or they may drift further on the next season.

They may have a relationship, or they may insist that they don't believe in dating or belonging to a single person. If they are in a relationship, it is one that is either considered 'open' or they go around cheating on each other. Drugs, most often pot, are a constant in their life, and they use alcohol like it is water.

All of this they do under the guise that they are a 'free spirit'. No one is going to tell them what to do, they aren't going to be bound by rules or structure, and they certainly aren't going to listen to any authority figure... whether that figure be a boss, the government, or their own parents.

Sound familiar? No doubt it is. This kind of person is everywhere, and always has been. They proclaim themselves to be free, and they lie to themselves telling themselves that they are free, when they are really more enslaved than anyone else.

Through the ages, it has always been popular among young people (especially people in their teens) to do what they want. It is considered the 'cool' thing to do if you have no responsibility and you don't show up for things that you are supposed to go to.

You don't do your chores, you don't go to school, you don't even show up for work. You're one of the 'cool' kids.

Sadly, this is a trend that has taken grip on society as a whole. It is no longer a phase that kids go through, it is a way of life that a lot of adults embrace. They aren't going to work because they don't want to, they aren't going to follow the law because they don't agree with it.

They aren't going to follow a proper and nutritious diet because they say that they only live once, and that they are going to live it up while they can. They cheat on their partners. They do harmful things to their bodies. All in the name of freedom.

They think that they have life all figured out, and no one can tell them what to do or what not to do. They are in charge, they have life all figured out, and they are free.

Right?

Wrong.

Never think that you can achieve total enlightenment or attain complete awareness if you are not willing to work for it.

In other words, you have to drop your ego.

It is not at all uncommon for us to think that we have life all figured out. For most, they don't think that they need to meditate or view life in light of there being something more or something deeper.

Most people go through life thinking that they have it all figured out in their own minds, and they know what they need to do to be happy. Of course, what they are doing to be happy doesn't make them happy, so they try new things, or they do more of the things that they are already doing, but this only ends in loss of jobs, unhappy and broken relationships, money problems, health problems, and the list goes on.

The harsh truth is that you *don't* have life all figured out. Life is full of choices, actions, and consequences. You might think that you are able to see through it all, and that these things don't apply to you. You might think that you really are free in spite of all the evidence to the contrary, but you can only lie to yourself and others for so long.

Your life is a result of your choices. If you want to continue in a life of slavery and bad endings, continue in the path you have chosen. If you want to see it grow and change, you have to be willing to make a difference, and you do need to put in the work.

"You need to make a conscious effort to channel your life energies and your thoughts into the light. If you do not, you are going to constantly be pushed backwards into darkness."

It is a sad thing to think, but it's true. If you aren't making a deliberate effort on a daily basis to point your energy into something that is better and higher, you are only going to be sinking further back. And the way to channel this energy is to have the discipline to practice it.

You are constantly putting out energy into the world. What you are doing is directing where your life is going, and it is going to continue to direct where your life goes. If you sit back and do nothing so to speak, what you are really doing is continuing on a path that isn't good, and a path that is going to carry you further and further away from your goals.

You are either going one way or the other. If you make bad choices, or if you make no choices at all, you are going to tend towards the negative side of things, but if you consciously make an effort to do better, and to further where you are in life, you are going to see your life take a turn for the better, and continue on that path.

But I don't believe it. I have lived so many years doing my own thing, and I have gotten along just fine in life. Sure, I would like to make some more money, or maybe lose some weight, but besides that I have life all together.

It is not uncommon for people to argue the fact that they need discipline. They think that they do have life under control, and that they are in charge of their desires.

They assume that bad things happen to everyone, and everyone on this planet assumes that they are the ones with the worst luck of anybody. You assume that you just happened to lose your job because *bad things happen*.

Your partner or spouse just up and left you because *bad things happen*.

You struggle with health problems or money problems because *bad things happen*.

And, it is true. Bad things *do* happen, but these aren't the bad things that just happen to you. Sure, you might end up sick without a given cause, but those cases are rare. More often than not, all of these things happen because of something that you were doing.

You were the one that lost your job when the company downsized because of the effort you put forth at work. You fight with your partner because you don't agree on most things, but you refuse to put forth the effort to finding a partner you are suitable for. You don't budget your money so you end up in debt.

See what I mean? Most of the 'bad things' that 'just happen' in life, are usually a direct result of the poor choices that you are making right now.

Most people assume that if they don't have a problem with drugs and alcohol then they are in complete control of their desires, but I want to share with you a scenario that is going to show you how your desires can take root no matter what it is.

Learning Example 1:

You decide that you need to go to the gym. You don't like how you look in the mirror, or perhaps you want to attract someone that is fit and attractive themselves.

So, you go through the hoops, you buy a gym membership, you buy the clothes that you need, and you head out.

But then reality hits.

Working out is hard. It is uncomfortable (at least for most people).

You work at it for a week. For two weeks, and you see minimal results if any.

So what do you do? You become lazy. You go to the gym less, and you eventually stop going at all.

Then you get fatter. Your back starts to hurt, so you go to the doctor, and he tells you that you are starting to develop health problems. Perhaps you have high cholesterol. Or you have a cyst somewhere in your body.

You know that you need to lose weight, and this time your motivation is fueled by your need to improve your health, so you go back to the gym. But it is once again uncomfortable.

Now, you don't want to go back to the doctor because you don't want to hear that something else with your health is failing, but you also don't want to go back to the gym because you don't like how that feels, either.

You become enslaved in a circle that drives you both to the gym and away from the gym all at once. Of course, you are ruled by your desires, so you go to the gym because you want to, but then you don't go to the gym because you don't want to. Yet the problem is worsening all around. Your health is failing and you dislike how you look in the mirror more and more.

You might think that you have the freedom to do what you want all the time, but you can see here that it is only making your life worse.

You have become trapped by your own desires.

When this happens, it is a lot easier to push the blame on other things, and wonder why you are the victim of so many bad things that happen to you, but as you can see here, it is a direct result of the choices that you are making.

If you want to turn your life around, you have to make the choice to change it, and you have to focus your energy and make a conscious effort to stick with those changes, even if it hurts.

Chapter 5 – Are You Really Free... Really?

I know this all sounds bleak when you hear it for the first time, and I know that you only feel more and more trapped the more you realize that you got yourself into this life that you are living.

But, along with the desire to help you realize the root of your problems, I also have the desire to help you get out of your problems, I want you to succeed, and I want you to get out of the struggles and hardships you are in the midst of.

I am going to help you get there, but first I want to help you realize why this ends up being a vicious cycle you are trapped in. Back to the gym learning exercise. In this example, we are imagining that you have health problems because you refuse to go to the gym, but then when you go to the gym to rid yourself of health problems, you find that it is also painful.

So what is the most common thing that you do?

You embrace denial. You embrace the victim mentality.

In short, you run.

You are afraid to go to the gym because of the pain that it causes, and you are afraid to not go to the gym because of the pain that decision causes as well. So you end up going back and forth and back and forth, one decision to the other, always running.

You are running from the decision that causes you the most pain at the time, which is always changing.

Let's turn this back around to the freedom that you claim that you have. You are free to not go to the gym, because that is a choice that is up to you. You are free to not go back to the doctor, well, because no one can make you go to the doctor.

So you are free to not take care of your health, and you are free to not check up on your health... but as you can clearly imagine this only means that your health is going to get worse.

Your weight is going to go up, your energy is going to go down. You will experience more problems and more issues, and you are going to find that it hurts more and more to do even the most simple of things. You may be forced to quit your job due to your health problems, and you may even lose your partner due to your poor health choices, and your refusal to take care of yourself.

Does this sound like freedom to you?

Of course not. This is a perfect example of how you are controlled by your desires. You make the choices based on what you wanted at the time, but you are forced to live with the consequences that came from those choices.

Now, you are stuck in the cycle of bad. You can't make the choice that you want to make because you are too busy avoiding the pain that goes along with it. All the while this is getting worse and worse, and you can't make choices that you used to make because those are becoming painful to do as well.

With this kind of mindset and this kind of life, you can't go out and be a creator, because you are stuck where you are in a wheel. You are just like a hamster that is always running and running in its cage, but can't ever get anywhere because you are just running in circles.

You have to realize that any dream, whether that be weight, health, money, a relationship, a business position... anything worth having... you can't have unless you are willing to put a lot of work into it.

In order to do this you are going to need to develop a system of self-discipline. It is the only way that you are going to get what you want in life, live life, and succeed in your goals and dreams.

Cause and effect. Every choice that you make can and does have consequences. That is a truth that you need to accept, and it is a truth that you need to embrace. I know that when you read it in the sense of the example up above that it sounds bad, but you can change that all around.

Bad choices lead to bad outcomes, but if you do work hard, and you do put in the effort, you are going to get consequences for those actions as well. You are going to lose the weight, you are going to get the partner that you want, and you are going to succeed at work.

And the root to all of this is a well-rounded cycle of self-discipline.

Now don't misunderstand me, I am not saying that you need to be hard on yourself, or that you need to always criticize yourself. That is once again pulling up the negative connotation that hangs on to the word 'discipline'. Although there are definite times when you do need to be hard on yourself and make a change for the better, I am talking about and easier kind of self-discipline, but discipline just the same.

As soon as you develop a system of self-discipline for yourself, and you get on that straight and narrow path towards your goal, you are going to find an entirely new life.

You are going to feel stress lifted off of your shoulders and taken away, you are going to find fulfillment in your choices and in your day. You are going to start to see those good results that you have been spending so much time hunting for.

The more habits you set up in your life, the more you are going to want to have those habits in place.

What seems to be so constricting right now is really the key to your ultimate sense of freedom.

This is because you are morphing out of being a puppet that is tossed this way and that by your desires, and into a creator that is continuously changing and growing. Think of this idea as an investor, and you are investing so much wealth and value in yourself that you can't help but grow all the more from it.

The more stock you put into yourself, the more you are going to *want* to work. There is a delicate balance here, because these are things that you can put into yourself right now, but they are going to take some time to build.

I know that you are struggling right now with the fear that this is just a ploy to get you into something that you can't get out of, but I promise you that if you are willing to put in the work, in five, ten, or fifteen years down the road you are going to be able to look back and see how far you have come, and you are going to be amazed.

You are going to find a sense of fulfillment, excitement, and happiness that there is no way you can feel right now. You are going to learn that you do have a choice. Because when you are at that point in your life, you really will have a choice.

But I have a choice right now...

You think that, or you say that, but do you?

Do you have a choice of whether you work at your job or not?

Do you have to be there for any reason?

If you have to be there for any reason, whether it be for something so simple as needing the money, then you don't have the freedom that you think you have.

Have you put in the work into your career so far that you can decide whether you work at the job you are currently working at or not? Do you have to set aside the things that you really do want to pursue because you are stuck at a job that just pays the bills?

Odds are, you don't have that freedom. This isn't a surprise, however, as a lot of people don't have that freedom. Most people really do get up and go to work at their jobs simply because they do need the money, and that job they have is how they are going to get the money, whether they like the job or not.

People who get up, go to work, and stay at a simple nine to five kind of job feel that they don't have a lot of options when it comes to where they can work. They say that they don't have time to look for jobs, or they don't have the time to go apply for other jobs.

Many of them don't even realize what it is that they want to do, because they spend their days going to work and going home. In and out. That's it.

If you were to start your own business, or pursue the career of your dreams, you would feel as though you had options, but the problem is that causes you to have to work. To have to make changes that are different and uncomfortable, or changes that are downright hard.

This is why so many people stay stuck. Change is hard, and they don't want to do anything that could be considered hard.

But let's move on.

Are you free in your relationships?

Are you free to leave the person you are with right now?

Are you free to go out into the world and attract the life mate that you want?

If your immediate inclination is to say yes, I want to challenge you to stop and think for a moment.

If that is true, then why are you still with the person that you are with? Of course if you are happy with who you are with then that is the answer, but if you feel that you are free to go out there and get the mate that you do want, are you really happy with the mate that you currently have?

Have you built yourself up enough to make the choices that you need to make to find the partner that you want to have, or are you just stuck in the relationship that you are in because it is easy?

Sure, you say that you care about them or you don't want to hurt them, or you can't be alone, but those are never good reasons to be in a relationship you are not happy with. If you wanted to be with them, then you wouldn't give thought about finding someone else, and if you want to find someone else, then you ought to have the guts to do what you need to do to make that happen.

Unfortunately, many people shy away from the work that is involved to do these things. They make excuses, and they feel stuck. They don't want to put in the work to make those things happen, and they end up wasting their lives because they choose the easy way out of things.

If you were to work on yourself, to develop the things that you like and don't like, to work out and make yourself more attractive to the opposite sex, to have goals and be reaching for them... you would have options.

Instead, you plunk your way through life and refuse to work on yourself, or to do anything that is uncomfortable, and as a result you end up with the person that you don't really want, just a person who is happy... or at least tolerates... you.

You might argue that you are happy with your current relationship, but I have to say that I bet if you had options out there, and I mean real options, that you would be a lot more likely to explore those options rather than stay where you are and who you are with.

And the same goes back with the job. If you had your dream job offered to you, it is highly unlikely you would turn it down because you are free at the job you currently have. You would take it in a heartbeat. The only issue is that this job isn't going to be offered to you because you aren't doing anything to make that happen.

This isn't just talking about jobs and relationships, it spills over into your position at work, your weight, your health, or whatever your goal in life happens to be.

Chapter 6 – Freedom is an Option, and is Found Within Options

Now, when many people hear what I said in the last chapter spoken to them, they take one of two stances. They are either insistent that they really are happy exactly where they are, and they hold fast to the fact that they think they have real freedom...

Or,

They feel sorry for themselves and proclaim that they are stuck where they are, they are unhappy, and that they can't make the change that they want to make for one reason or another.

Denial and self-pity are two factors that reign supreme in the world that we live in. It is hard to admit that life isn't as you would want it to be, so you refuse to admit that, and it is hard to accept that you got yourself into this mess, so you can get yourself back out of it.

If you had either of these two responses you are among many, but even if you didn't, you are still going to need some direction as to where you are going to take all of this.

Even if you are excited about making a change, and more than willing to accept responsibility, I want to help you. I think that it is great that you are willing to take on this challenge head on, and that you have the confidence to admit when you make a mistake and be willing to change that mistake that you made, but I don't want you to end up as you were again.

Focus and guided direction is going to take you exactly where you need to be in your life.

There can be a lot of excitement with the concept of change, but there can also be a lot of fear. You may be feeling excited, fearful, or just downright stuck, but before we can move forward with all of this, we need to clean out your closet a bit further.

True freedom means that you are creating options for yourself.

As you can see by that statement alone, the definition of you being truly free means that you are going to be able to make changes when you want to make them, because you have the ability to do that.

You have options.

Now, this is a wonderful thing to have, but true freedom requires a lot of work to achieve. As a rule of thumb, people don't just give you a lot of options. You have to be the one that is out there in the real world, fighting for them.

Right now, you have to admit to yourself that you are a slave.

Now, hang on just a second. You are not going to shift your thinking into blame. You are not a slave to your boss, or to your job, you are not a slave to food, or to your significant other.

You are a slave to yourself, and to your own desires.

Look around yourself, you are a slave to everything that is around you. You may try to blame your slavery on other things. You think that you are a slave to yourself, or to your partner in your relationship, or your schedule, but the fact of the matter is that all of these things come back full circle to your own desires. If you are completely honest with yourself, and you examine the problem at the root of the problem, you are going to see that your desires are at the root of this.

So what is the answer? How can you break out of your slavery to yourself?

Work.

You need to work on yourself.

I know that doesn't sound fun, and as a general rule of thumb we would all take the easy life over what is hard. After all, why wouldn't you want to spend your day at home playing video games? That sounds easy.

And it is easy, for now, but you can't escape the problems that are going to come from this pain later on, and you are going to have to deal with the consequences. There is just no way around that.

You say that you know you need to work on yourself, which is obviously true as you purchased this book to make that happen, so let's break this down into how you can get your true freedom.

It is likely that by now discipline and work are pretty interchangeable in your vocabulary. You know that you need to work on disciplining yourself and that in itself is an attitude of discipline.

But the end result to both of these things is the creation of options for yourself, and that is where your true freedom lies.

Chapter 7 – Willpower 101

I know that this has all been a lot to digest, and that by now your head is probably spinning. You are feeling empowered, and like you are ready to take on the world, but there is something that you are going to have to watch out for.

This is something that you have likely dealt with in the past, and it is something that is going to continue to pop up in your life from time to time

The "who cares" attitude.

It may seem funny that I am bringing this up right now, but that is because I want you to stay focused in your discipline, and I want you to achieve your goal of total freedom. I want you to be free, and I don't want you to give up when the going gets tough and you don't feel like trying anymore.

That is where willpower is going to come in.

Before we get into what willpower actually is, let's take a minute to establish what it is not.

So many people assume that willpower is a lot of talent being put into work, but that could not be further from the truth. Willpower has nothing to do with talent, and it has nothing to do with skills. It does, however, have everything to do with focus.

Society has always been in awe of people with talent. Through the ages, the message has been that all of the great painters, businessmen, musicians, classical artists, sculptors and so on have all been born with this great talent that you couldn't ever possibly hope to have.

This is a lie that society has sold to you to keep you small. Genius, or talent, is a practice. It is something that has to be worked on with discipline and continued practice rather than something that is just bestowed upon someone. Genius is not genetic and talent is not anything more than someone who had a lot of practice at what they are doing.

Don't believe me? Well let's take a look at a couple of the people that society has put on a pedestal as some of the greatest geniuses of the world:

1. Michelangelo is known for being one of the greatest painters that has ever lived.

It is true that he did paint the Sistine Chapel, and that his work is far beyond what anyone could have expected, but Michelangelo was not a painter. He was a sculptor. He had been pushed into creating the Sistine Chapel paintings by the pope of the day, and he spent 4 years, working nearly around the clock to make his work a masterpiece.

He worked so hard on this for so long that he suffered permanent eye damage as well as permanent damage to his back.

2. Mozart was not someone who loved music from the beginning.

His father was a piano teacher, and it fell to him to help carry on the family legacy to help bring home some form of income. Experts have studied him, and the music that he produced in the beginning had no inkling of genius to it, but rather was mere curiosity.

Through all of the time and dedication that he did to music, he grew into the classical artist that we know him for, but that was not his intention in the beginning, and that was not what it looked like was going to happen to him.

I could go on and on about different sports players, musicians, businessmen, and so on, but I think you get my point. In the society that we live in today, we are all jacks-of-all-trades. We never become a master of anything because we don't have the drive or the focus to become a master of anything.

These two men and countless others have all displayed a remarkable amount of willpower in their lives, and that is how they got to where they are today, whether it be in our present day lives, or in the history books where they are going to forever stand.

We love to think of people as being born with some sort of remarkable talent that helped them out of the poverty they were born into, but that is just not how it works.

Success is not inherited. It is built and it is earned.

This can be a hard truth to swallow, because this puts you to blame for where you are in life today. You are where you are because of the choices that you made. You are living the life you have settled to live.

It makes us feel better to think that we are a victim of our circumstances, but that is just not the case. You made the choice to live where you live, work where you work, be in a relationship with your partner, not exercise, and so on.

If you are not successful in life, this isn't a fun thing to hear, but don't worry, you are not alone. There are countless people in the same situation that you are in, and there are countless people that were in that situation, and came out of it even stronger and better than they ever thought that they could be.

You got yourself to where you are today, and you can get yourself out of it, too. You can take yourself so much higher and further and faster, you just have to have the willpower to do it. Success isn't a handout given to some lucky people, you make your own success and you earn your own genius.

Chapter 8 – How to Live a Successful Life: Part 2

It is mind boggling to think that you can have the successful life that you want. Your entire life, you have been fed the lie that you are 'normal' and the successful people that you see on the television or that you have read about in your history books are the people that are 'exceptional'.

As you have learned, this couldn't be further from the truth, and there is nothing at all remarkable about these people outside of their driven willpower and exquisite self-discipline.

In the next chapter, we are going to get into how you can develop greater willpower for yourself, and what you can do to apply that willpower to your life today, but right now, I want to show you the 5 principles about the rules of success.

These are principles that are going to change the way you view the successful, and empower you to become successful yourself. I know that we have already looked at the first one in detail, but I want to include it in this list because it is so very important for you to know.

1. Genius is practice.

Experts have done all kinds of research on the human mind and performance, and what they have discovered is that in order for a person to perform an activity at a genius level, they need to practice that same activity for a minimum of 10 years, or at least 10,000 hours.

Most people will try something out for a few weeks, then they will give up. They get bored or they don't see the results that they want to see, and they walk away from it, but what the experts have discovered is that it takes so much longer than that. We aren't even talking about weeks or months, but years longer to start performing at a level that is considered to be genius.

On the flip side of this discovery, you now have the proven assurance that you can be a genius at whatever you want to be, it is just going to take you hours upon hours of dedicated practice.

You need to do more than just practice, you need to practice deliberately.

This means that you can work on something a little bit every day for 10 years, and you are going to still be at a great level, but in order to get to genius level, you have to deliberately practice.

Deliberate practice is a practice that seeks to learn and get better. You consciously watch yourself perform one day, then the next day you try harder to perfect the part of your practice that wasn't as good as it could have been.

This means that the next day you are going to do better, then the next day you are going to do better still, then the next day, and the next. You see, this isn't just getting out the piano book and plunking your way through a song for half an hour a day for ten years, this is dedicated, hours a day practice that has the goal of doing better in mind.

Put yourself in good company.

It is all too true that like creates like. With this in mind, choose your friends carefully, and look for people that are the same as you are. Look for people with the end goal of being a genius at something.

You are going to find that you are a lot more motivated if you are surrounded by people that are also motivated, and you are going to be a lot more likely to stick with your newfound challenge if you are surrounded by people that are also working on their own level of genius.

2. You are going to grow when you aren't comfortable.

Society tells you that if you are feeling uncomfortable, that something is wrong. You are told to never challenge yourself or to rock your boat.

I am going to tell you straight, however, that if you are not scared, and if you are not working painfully hard on something, then you are not growing. You have to go through discomfort if you want to grow, that is just the way it is.

When you push your boundaries, your boundaries are going to move out further, and you are going to be able to reach further to get to them again.

You need to commit to your fear.

Face your fears head on, because the seduction of safety is more dangerous than the perception of uncertainty. When you are where you are comfortable, you aren't going to change.

Even if you want to change, you are going to stay stuck where you are because you think that is where things are going to be ok. The problem with this is that you aren't ever going to reach your goals this way, because you are always going to be stuck where you are.

3. **It is your responsibility to be great.**

If you are going to take all of this information and walk away from it, you are cheating your friends, your family, and yourself. If you are going to fall into the trap of thinking that you are 'ordinary' or 'normal' and not try to break out of it or further yourself, then you are cheating your own integrity.

It is your actual responsibility as a human being to make the most out of your life. You need to surround yourself with people who are also trying to better themselves, and you need to be reaching for the stars.

To do anything less than this is to settle for second best, and it is cheating the world out of what could be another genius added to the list of people that have made their mark on this planet.

Full expression of your willpower is the key to happiness.

Right now you might think spending all of your time watching television dramas is what is going to make you happy, or if you can spend your day with video games and pot you are going to never have a problem in the world, but consider this thought:

Ordinary people seek entertainment, extraordinary people invest in their learning. The greatest of the greatest are out there reaching. You don't ever see a truly successful person out there that is sitting home doing nothing. We aren't wired that way.

Dopamine, which is the chemical in the brain that produces happiness, is only produced by the brain when we do something great. It doesn't need to be anything great by the world's standards, but you aren't going to experience that rush of dopamine by sitting at home playing on your computer, you are going to get it by getting out there and doing something for yourself.

4. **The goal is the process.**

Don't get too focused on your end goal right now. Your goals are great, and they are very much worth having, but you don't want to get so focused on the end goal that you lose out on the process.

There is so much shaping and so much happiness that is found in working towards your goal, you are going to enjoy the journey as much if not more than you are going to enjoy actually achieving your goal.

If you do any studies on the geniuses of the past, you are going to see that they all loved what they were doing. Mozart didn't love being a great pianist, he enjoyed the music. Thomas Edison didn't love the fact that he invented the lightbulb, he loved doing the inventing process.

You need to reach the point in your life where you fall in love with the season of life that you are in, and right now, that is going to be the season of process. If you have been paying attention, you realize that there is never going to be a point in which you arrive in life. There is always going to be something else that is worth your pursuing and attention.

This means that you need to prepare your life as a life of growth, and one that is going to keep changing and molding into what is coming next.

5. **The secret of all great success relies in change.**

If you want to be known for greatness, you need to change your perspective on it. In order to be great, you need to make a habit of doing small wins often, rather than one large win once in your life.

You are going to change into someone that is great, not something that did something great that one time.

Small daily improvements over time grow into beautiful success.

If you take a look at any of the geniuses that you read about in history, or even the great performers that we have today, there isn't one of them that had one single incident that made them successful.

These are all things that needed to be built and worked on over time. Amazon and Google didn't explode overnight. Lady Gaga and Taylor Swift didn't just pop up out of nowhere.

These and countless others like them are things that took a lot of time and patience, but most of all, work. You didn't just hear one day of a performer that was great, if you were paying attention, you would have seen them rise to that greatness.

There are so many people out there that want a quick fix plan. They want to excuse themselves for where they are in their lives, and they want to have their success handed out to them right here and right now, but that just isn't going to happen.

If you want to be successful, you are going to have to work for it. You can't have the partner you want, or the job that you want, or the body that you want by doing what you are doing right now, you have to get up off of your couch and get out there and work for those things.

This is going to take discipline and it is going to take willpower, but you have plenty of both right at your fingertips.

Chapter 9 – The Science of Willpower

To this point, I have been talking a lot about self-discipline, but I have mentioned that willpower has a lot to do with it. If you want to be able to achieve that discipline, you are going to need to have the willpower to do it. The two of them go hand in hand.

Now, let's get into the ins and outs of willpower. Let's take a look at what it is and what it's all about. In essence, let's take a look at the science behind it all.

1. **Willpower is like a muscle rather than an inherited quality.**

   Nobody is born with great willpower. The people that you see that are 'hardcore' or are dedicated to the things that they are doing, are people that took the time to develop that willpower over the course of time.

There is absolutely no difference between you and the person you see jogging in the snow at 5 o'clock in the morning. It is a complete myth to say that some people are 'morning people' and some people aren't.

You can build willpower just the same as you build muscle.

Scientists have studied the brain multiple times, learning things and figuring things out, and what they have learned is that the brain can grow and change right along with the rest of you.

You don't have the same brain that you were born with, you have the brain that you have earned. Scientists have seen with their own eyes that the section of the brain that houses our ability to have willpower actually changes and grows as we develop a stronger willpower in the world around us.

The fixed brain theory is a myth.

It has been proven time and time again that the brain can grow and change in ways that you want it to, and that you are able to mold it into what you want it to be.

Just like you can mold and sculpt your muscles to look like you want them to look, you can train your brain to develop in the way that you want it to work.

The 3 week rule is also a myth.

We have all heard and have grown up with the thought that it takes 3 weeks to develop a new habit. If you want to do something, it is going to be 3 weeks of hard work, and after that it is going to just be a habit that is going to come easily to you.

This, my friend, is a myth. It takes not 21 days, but rather 66 days before something actually sets in as a fixed new habit. This is more than 3 times as long as we originally thought, but there is actual science to back that up.

We start something, and we stick with it for 5 days or so, but then it becomes uncomfortable and we give up. This is because your brain is wired to want to do things the other way. It takes literal re-wiring of your brain to instill a new habit, which is why it is so hard to do so.

2. **The more choices you make, the less willpower you will have.**

Think of it this way, you have a fixed amount of willpower in a day, and the more choices you make, the less willpower you have for the next choice.

It is a proven fact that we as people make our worst choices between 10 at night and midnight. This is because you have spent all of your willpower during the day making all kinds of different choices, so by the time you get to that point at night, you don't have any willpower left to make a good decision.

So if you are using willpower on things that aren't important, then you are wasting willpower that you can use on other, more important things.

Scientists ran a study in which people who had to make a lot of choices were put in a room with people that only needed to make a few choices.

Both groups needed to put their hands in bowls of cold water, and it was proven that the people that made the more choices were unable to keep their hands in the water as long as the people that didn't have as many choices to make.

3. **Self-Awareness is the DNA of transformation.**

Between every moment, there is ¼ second of silence. For every piece of cake that is offered and your response, for every temptation and your reaction, for every cause and effect, you have a ¼ second window of opportunity.

The more you can become aware of yourself, and the more you can have awareness in general, the more control you are going to have over these situations. You really can develop more gray matter in your brain, and develop an ability to make better choices in this quarter of a second.

If scientists were able to study willpower, were they also able to give us ways to increase willpower in our own lives?

Thankfully, the answer is yes. There are very specific and clear things that you can do starting right now that is going to increase your willpower and help you develop it even further on down the road.

1. **Meditate**

   Meditation is a practice that I can't recommend enough. The more you do it, the more you are going to benefit from it. I wish that I could get everyone I come in contact with to meditate for at least an hour a day, but even if you don't, even if you only meditate for 15 minutes in a day, you are going to increase your willpower exponentially.

We as people were designed to meditate. It is good for our bodies, and it is good for our minds. Science has proven that meditation really does increase the size of the frontal cortex in your brain, and with the increase of that, you are going to see an increase of willpower.

Make a deliberate effort, starting today, to spend some time in meditation.

2. **Exercise**

Physical exercise has so many benefits it is hard to believe that they are all true. Experts say that exercise is the wonder drug for willpower, and that those that exercise for just a few minutes every day have more than double the willpower than those that refuse to exercise at all.

I am not saying that you have to go out there and become a marathon runner, all you need to do is incorporate a level of exercise into your day, and you will see a difference. It is how our minds are set up. It is impossible for you to start exercising and not see a real and positive difference in this realm.

3. **Sleep**

Sleep is where all too many people fall short. We think that we don't have time to sleep like we should, or we are really just too lazy to go to bed on time.

It is vitally important for you to get enough sleep, for your health, and for your self-discipline. Science has proven that those who are getting enough sleep, at least 7 hours of sleep in a night, are able to display tons more willpower than those that are not getting enough sleep.

It has been scientifically shown that people that are tired or not getting enough sleep are far more likely to cave into temptations, and are far more likely to have cravings than those that are getting enough sleep.

Just like you may need to set an alarm to get up in the morning, you also need to make an effort to go to bed on time. This is the only way you are going to ensure that you getting enough sleep at night.

I wish that there was an easy way to just have willpower, but there isn't. If you want to have defined muscles, you have to go to the gym and lift weights. It is going to take time, and it is going to be hard, but if you are dedicated to going to the gym, and you are determined to stick with it, you are going to end up with the defined muscles that you want.

The same goes for your willpower. If you want to have a lot of willpower, you are going to have to exercise it and work on it. You are going to have to do things that are uncomfortable, and you are going to have to work at it until you are able to do it, then you are going to have to push yourself further.

As you can see, self-discipline and willpower are virtually the same thing. Yes, there are differences that separate them, and there are things that are going to keep them different, but overall, you are going to use them and acquire them at the same time and in the same ways.

Chapter 10 – Putting it all Into Practice: Developing Self-Discipline and Willpower

By this point, I know that you have a thorough understanding of what I have been talking about, and you know that you have to do a lot of work to get willpower as well as self-discipline, and that those things are just the beginning.

You know that once you develop your willpower, then you are going to have to use that willpower to make the changes in your life that you want to make. Just because you have greater willpower, it doesn't mean that all of your problems are going to disappear, you are just going to have a better way of dealing with your problems than you did before.

But I don't want to overwhelm you, so let's just focus on developing good willpower right now. What are the practical and tactical things that you can do that are going to help you develop greater willpower and self-discipline?

These things are simple to do, they are just going to require that you do them.

1. **Get plenty of rest in your day.**

   Now, I am not talking about taking a nap or shutting everything off, but what I mean is that you need to take a break. Take some time to re-group and refocus, then go back to work with a vigor.

   Experts recommend that you work for 90 minutes, then you take a 10 minute rest. You need to work as hard as you can for the 90 minutes, then you don't worry at all about it for the 10 minutes.

This is how you are going to work through your entire day. You are going to give it your absolute all for those 90 minutes, then you aren't going to worry about it for those 10 minutes, then you are going to get right back to it for 90 more minutes.

Take one day a week for total rest and total recovery.

This is an entire day in the week when you aren't going to touch your computer, your television, or anything that is electronic. You aren't going to work on anything, and you aren't going to stress. You are going to enter into complete and total recovery, and you are going to leave it at that.

This is going to clear your mind in ways that you never thought possible. We think in this world that we live in that we can't go a day without technology.

We have to always have our phones and our computers, our televisions and our tablets.

We think that if we put them down for even an hour we are going to miss out on something that is life changing and phenomenal, but I promise you that this is not the case. Even 50 years ago, there was no such thing as a cell phone, and computers were so big and heavy no one had one.

Televisions weren't anything like they are today, and you didn't need to have any kind of social media to feel fulfilled. That is because these are just things that add stress and pressure to you, and that is stress and pressure that you don't need.

It is only for 1 day out of a whole week, and after a couple of weeks of doing this, you are going to be thankful for that day in your week. You aren't going to miss it, and you aren't even going to want it.

Every 6 weeks, take an entire weekend off (or more if you can).

I know that this sounds like a lot, but you are going to love how good you feel when you get out of your life for a while. Even when you love your life, you need to take a moment to step back and analyze what you have, and appreciate what you have.

Clear your mind and come back into play with full focus. There is so much that you can do with your life when you are full of willpower, so don't be afraid to take some time off.

2. **Get some kind of physical exercise into your day.**

I know that I mentioned this already in the last chapter, but I am saying it again here because it is that important. We as people are made to move. Get up and out of the house, or do an exercise video in the house.

Work up a sweat and transform your body. If that is your goal with this book anyway, you are going to be happy with this one, but if it isn't, you are going to benefit from this anyway.

It doesn't matter what this exercise is, you just need to get up and move for 20 minutes in your day. Many experts say that you ought to do this first thing in your day, but that is up to you. If you aren't able to do it first thing in your day, then just do it when you can.

As long as you are exercising, you are going to see the benefits and you are going to feel the increase in your willpower.

3. **Make "I CAN" the biggest part of your vocabulary.**

You have no idea how powerful your words are. The more you tell yourself that you can't, the more you won't be able to. You are going to think the way that you treat yourself, and if you are always telling yourself and others that you can't do it, then you are going to be the one who can't do it.

You have to increase the amount of positive phrases in your vocabulary, and cut back on the negative ones.

4. **Be a deliberate minimalist.**

Doing big things in life is less important than not doing other things in life. In other words, saying 'no' is just as important as it is to say yes. You need to learn how to focus your life on 1 or 2 things, and spend your energies on that.

Simplify. Make your life about the little things, and practice deliberate minimalism. Instead of trying to master 30 things, try to only do 1. Instead of having a huge group of friends, work on having 1 great friend.

The more that you bring into your life, the less energy you are going to have to focus on any one thing. You need to simplify and cut out the distractions. Figure out what it is you want, and go for that one thing.

5. **Pick your friends carefully.**

We become like the people that we are around. That is the simple fact of the matter, and it is a truth that you can't escape. You are most like the people you spend most of your time with.

If you are around gossips, you are a gossip. If you are around victims, you are a victim. It has been this way since the beginning of time, but it is time to break out of that.

You want to be better than that, so it is time that you start choosing better than that. You are going to be like the people you spend most of your time around, so get in with the crowd of people that are going somewhere.

6. **Keep a clean environment.**

Let minimalism take over your life. Clear out the clutter and get rid of the extra things that are hanging around. The less that you have to work around, the more productive you are going to be.

Mess creates stress.

It is a proven fact that the more mess you have around your home, the less willpower you are going to have. You need to get rid of the clutter that is in your home, and you are going to see that it also gets rid of the clutter that is in your mind.

The things that are lying around you do have an effect on you, so pick the up and tidy them up. You can do it, and you are going to see that it increases your willpower when you do.

So what's next?

I know that this has all been a lot of information for you, and that you are now on the path to making some great changes in your life, but now lies the question, "what is the next step? How are you going to sustain all of this and use it to make a difference in your life?"

Well, to put it simply, you need to make the deliberate change. You can want to make the change, you can try to make the change, but until you actually make that change, you are going to struggle.

I don't want you to put this off anymore. You have the power to change right now, and you have it right in front of you. I have told you all of the key things that you need to do, so now all that remains is you doing it.

There is no quick fix here, and there isn't an easy way out. You need to change.

And there is no better time than right now.

Conclusion

Thank you again for downloading this book!

I hope this book was able to help you to achieve self-discipline in your schedule, and develop the willpower to keep moving forward.

The next step is to keep pressing on. I know that this is hard, and I am sure that you noticed the trend in the book is to keep working towards your dreams and your goals, but let me assure you, when you are willing to work for your dreams, you are going to achieve them.

The person that gives up is the person that never makes it. So no matter what you are trying to do, you can do it with the right amount of willpower. You might need to work at your schedule for a while, and practice to develop the self-discipline that you are going to need for this, but it is going to come.

One of the beautiful things about being human is the fact that we adapt. You can make your schedule seem a lot harder than what it is right now, but once you adapt to it, you are going to realize that it isn't as hard as you feared it would be, and that you are enjoying more free time now than you ever were before.

It is as though the tighter the ship you run, the more fun you are going to have, and the greater the success you are going to achieve. Always remember that you have to work for this, and anything that you have to work for is going to take some time to achieve.

Never give up. This is a way of life, and it is going to be something that you are going to have to develop and get used to, but I assure you that it is a lot easier to get used to the success than it is to get used to the struggle that you are enduring right now.

As soon as you see where all of this is headed, and as soon as you see your dreams start to come true, you aren't going to give another thought to any of the hard work that is involved. It is all going to become such a second nature to you that it is going to feel like this is how you have always lived.

Finally, if you enjoyed this book, then I'd like to ask you for a favor, would you be kind enough to leave a review for this book on Amazon? It'd be greatly appreciated! I am a self published author and I would really need all help I can get. If you did not like the book, I would like to ask you to email me about what you thought I could have done better. email me at harveysegler@gmail.com

Just go to amazon and to your order history to find this book and then click "review this title".

And don't forget you free gift on the next side!

FREE Bonus!

Want to make money while you sleep?

Visit >>><u>www.GreenSleeper.com</u><<< to get free tips about how you can make serious money while doing anything else! Sleeping, laying on the beach, traveling, only your imagination is the limit!

At the moment you can get a FREE download of:

The "Make Money While You Sleep" Guide

But hurry up, the book will not be there forever!

Visit My Friends Website And Download It Now! 100% Free! What Do You Have To Lose? Just visit www.GreenSleeper.com.

If you don't want the book, read the blog which can teach you a lot of things about business, time management, performance and other things connected to business and success.

Thank you and good luck!

Made in United States
North Haven, CT
11 July 2022

21183171R00067